the I

Maurice Burns

Illustrated by Janet Duchesne

Ginn

From early morning, heavy showers moved across the farmland. A westerly wind forced the rain into every nook and cranny. The ground had soaked up its fill of water and was now gathering puddles. The hedgerows dripped and dripped.

In a field under a bush, crouched Tara the Ditch Cat. She was wet through, and feeling very miserable. The ditch was her home now, but at one time she'd had a much better life.

Tara looked out as a farmer turned his red tractor at the head of the field, and memories stirred inside her. She remembered a cosy warm basket by a gas fire. She remembered saucers of milk coming down from a table. Most of all, she remembered being brushed and stroked by loving human hands.

However, all that had changed when a strange man came to live in the house. He didn't like cats and certainly did not want one living in his house.

Late one evening, Tara was taken out of the house. She found herself in the back seat of a car, being driven out of the city and along country roads. As the comforting noise of traffic faded, Tara began to feel uneasy. At a quiet spot, the car stopped. The door was opened and the man waited.

After a few seconds, Tara finally realised he was waiting for her to get out. She did so, stepping slowly down into a strange new world. The car sped quickly off in the direction of the city.

As the red lights disappeared, Tara found herself in total darkness. The only things round her were the sounds and shapes of the night. Tara was a city cat, a house cat, a basket cat unused to being alone with the night. She did not know what to do. She crept off the road and curled up in the dry leaves at the bottom of a ditch.

Early the next morning, Tara padded along the road until she came to a farmhouse. Stepping into the farmyard, she was set upon by three angry farm cats. She turned and ran away as fast as she could go. She didn't stop until she was back in the safety of the ditch.

With a heavy heart she sighed, and started her life as a ditch cat.

Slowly she began to try to fend for herself. Her first attempts at hunting were hopeless. She was so slow and clumsy. For the first few days she ate very little and her sleek, plump, city-cat look soon disappeared.

However, her hunting gradually improved. Hungry days became a thing of the past and Tara grew much fitter.

In the summer, the ditch was full of mice and voles, rabbits and rats. The fields, too, were full of tasty things to eat. When the combine harvester had cut and cleared the fields, hunting was easy.

In winter, it was very different. All around, as far as Tara's sharp eyes could see, the countryside was covered with a thick blanket of snow. Tara would sit in her lonely ditch, looking out at a grey sky and watching the huge snowflakes settle.

It was beautiful, Tara admitted to herself, but it was bare, and food was difficult to find. She would shiver and wrap herself up more closely in her fur. She was proud of her thick, black coat and was glad of it in the cold winter weather.

At first she thought that she would not survive, but as she grew sharper and fitter, her fears lessened. The worst thing for her then was the loneliness. In the ditch world, there were no friends.

The grunting hedgehog only rolled himself into a ball as soon as Tara touched him.

The badger never even stopped. He just sniffed and moved on.

The stoat stopped and then dived away into the tall green grass.

Even the colourful adder hissed when Tara tried to play with his long tail.

There were no games to play and no friends to play with.

However, there was much to watch.

After several months, Tara's loneliness came to a dramatic end. On this particular day, the early morning rain had stopped and the countryside was gleaming in the afternoon sunshine. Tara was content. She had hunted well and she was purring softly. Perhaps she would have a nap and dream about her old life.

A long way off, the countryside was coming to life. Unfamiliar noises and smells made Tara stir in the ditch. Across the far fields, Tara could see horseriders in red tunics galloping this way and that. The hunt was on!

The noise of the horn echoed around the farm. Dogs yelped and ran about. They stopped, sniffed the ground and moved away. Always they kept their noses to the ground.

Tara spotted the quick, red fox scurrying across the field near her ditch. The dogs were on the scent. The riders were still a long way off.

The fox quickly made for the gap in Tara's ditch. Looking over his shoulder, he headed for the river. The dogs yelped as they tore across the field chasing the fox. They headed towards the hedge further up from Tara and forced themselves through it, squirming as they urged their bodies through.

Then all went quiet. Tara thought it was safe to come out. Without thinking, she left the ditch and came face to face with a foxhound.

Suddenly, Tara the Ditch Cat turned tiger. Her tail shot straight up. Her claws engaged. Hissing and spitting, she launched herself at the foxhound. Although he was taken by surprise, the foxhound was also full of fight. Growling and snarling, he defended himself.

The dog snapped and bit at the cat. The cat bit and tore at the dog. Round and round they went, like a Catherine-wheel. Neither would be the first to let go.

By now the riders were crossing the field. Shouting and slapping their horses, they rode for the gap. The noise of the riders and the sound of the horn distracted the foxhound. With one last snarl at the cat, he turned to rejoin the pack. Tara crawled back to the ditch in very poor shape.

In much pain, she lay under her bush, her sides rising and falling in rapid movements. The many cuts were sapping her strength. The countryside fell quiet again. A breeze moved over the rich grass and birds whistled along the ditch. The hunt was over the river by now. Tara closed her eyes and slept.

Further along the ditch, the children from the farm were blackberrying. With stained lips and hands, they bent and stretched to reach the fruit. One by one the juicy berries landed in the plastic cups with a ping. When each cup was full, it was emptied into the basket. The floor of the basket was nearly covered already. The children moved the basket along as they finished each bush. They were getting close to Tara, but Tara was too sore to notice or to care.

"Bring the basket over here, Danny," called Nina. "Just put it down there next to that stone."

Danny started to move, and then let out a yell. "Ugh! There's blood here. Look, Nina. It's everywhere!"

"Don't be so silly," called Nina over her shoulder. "Stop messing about and bring me the basket. My cup is spilling over with berries."

"I'm not messing about," Danny insisted. "Just come and look for yourself. Please!" There was something in his voice that made Nina get up at once.

Too weak to spit, Tara looked out from her ditch into the faces of the two children.

"Oh, you poor puss," whispered Nina. "You are in a bad way. Empty the basket, Danny," she ordered.

Danny looked at the basket, full of delicious, juicy berries. Then he looked at the cat, all bloody and scruffy. Finally, he looked back up at Nina.

"Come on, empty the basket," she ordered him again.

With mixed feelings, Danny did as he was told. The berries showered out onto the grass.

"The field-mice will have a picnic," he thought.

"Now, put your tracksuit top inside the basket," said Nina.

"Oh no, Nina, not my best tracksuit top!" he pleaded.

"Yes, Danny. This cat is in a bad way and, anyway, your top can be cleaned," said Nina.

Getting right down into the ditch, Nina bent and scooped up Tara. She placed her, ever so gently, into the basket. Tara's heart thumped violently when she felt the gentle hands lift her into the basket. She was too weak and ill to do anything but give one faint mew.

The children stepped over the blackberries on the floor and turned for home. With as little movement as possible, they made their way down the field, through the five-barred gate and onto the road.

Back at the farm they shouted for Mum.

"Are you back already?" she called, coming out of the chicken run. "That basket looks heavy! Did you get a lot? I expect I'll have enough for jam."

"Look what we found, Mum," called Danny.

Mum came over and peered into the basket.

"Oh dear," said Mum, "she looks in a bad way! Maybe the vet will have a look at her. She's here now, in the milking shed, seeing to the cows. What a bit of luck! Danny, run over to the shed and ask her to call in at the house before she leaves."

Nina and her mum took the basket inside.

The vet gently examined the cat as the children told the story of how they found her huddled in the ditch. While the vet was cleaning the open cuts, she discovered a thin chain around the cat's neck. It had been buried deep in the thick fur. The vet cut it with some pliers and found a small name tag.

"Well now," she said smiling. "This is no wild cat that you've found. She's obviously been loved at some time in her life, poor thing, though there's no doubt that she's a stray now."

She showed the tag to Nina and Danny. "Tara" it said.

When the vet had finished her examination, she gave Tara an injection.

"I think she might just pull through," she said hopefully. "But she'll need lots of TLC," she added, looking over her gold spectacles at the children.

There was a pause. "What's TLC? Is it the medicine in the bathroom?" asked Danny.

"No, no Danny," laughed Mum. "It means tender loving care."

The vet packed up her bag and went out to the car. "I'll call back in a few days," she called over her shoulder, "to see how Tara is coping." She closed her car door, and drove out of the yard.

Tara slept in a basket next to the fire. She never moved from her bed for a week. The children looked after her carefully, feeding her some milk every now and then from an old eye dropper. Tara would wake up, drink and fall asleep again. She slept for such a long time that the children worried in case she would never be well. But the tender loving care and the medicine were slowly helping her.

Then one morning, Nina and Danny came down and Tara was sitting up, staring at the fire. She ate some fish. She got up, stretched and walked round rubbing herself against everyone's legs. Then she went back to her basket next to the fire. She had, indeed, pulled through.

Each day Tara grew a little stronger. With all the TLC and the rich food, she soon recovered. Her cuts healed up, and her aches and pains went away. Her fur coat became thick and glossy again.

And, to Danny and Nina's great delight, Tara learned how to play again. Sometimes she would chase the table tennis ball when the children played. They would pretend to be cross, but they loved it when she took the ball away.

Sometimes she played with the laces in Danny's shoes,

or raced round the house chasing her tail.

When she grew tired, she would curl up in her basket and stare into the fire or listen to the wind whistling in the chimney top. Sometimes she would sit by the front door, looking out over the farm, like a king looking out over his kingdom.

The next step was not long in coming. As Mum came in from collecting eggs one day, Tara slipped out through the doorway and went for a walk on her own around the farmyard.

The air was fresh, filled with all the different sounds and smells of the farm. With her tail in the air, Tara padded around the farmyard looking in every doorway.

The horses looked down at her as she moved beneath the stable doors. Some ducks waddled past with their heads in the air. They went through a big puddle in front of the tractor shed. The old dog lay curled up on a sack near the barn door.

Tara crossed the farmyard in the direction of the milking shed. As she neared the doorway, she smelled danger.

Out bounded three spikey cats. Tara recognised them. They were the very same ones that had chased and scared her on her very first day in the country.

Things were different now. Tara was no longer the soft house cat she had been then. Now she was Tara the Ditch Cat. Arching her back, she spread her four legs wide. She snarled and spat. Her fur stood straight up as if charged with electricity. Her eyes stared at her old enemies.

"Come and try me," they seemed to say. "Who'll be first? Come on …"

The farm cats soon realised their mistake. First the white cat slunk away.

Then the tabby disappeared over the pigsty wall with a flash of her tail.

Only the ginger cat remained, and he stepped aside to let Tara into the milking shed.

Inside, a girl gave Tara some frothy warm milk on a cracked plate. Purring and lapping, Tara cleaned the plate. She gazed up at the great jars of milk above each cow.

Just then the children came running across the farmyard.

"Have you seen Tara?" they called out together.

"Oh, there she is," cried Danny.

"Here, puss. Come here, Tara," they called.

They bent down and petted Tara. They rubbed her and stroked her from the top of her head to the tip of her tail.

"Oh, thank goodness," whispered Nina. "We thought you had gone back to the ditch, Tara."

Tara looked up and her green eyes told Nina, "I'm not going anywhere! I'm staying here. I'm Tara the Farm Cat now, you know."